Answered Prayers

Also by Julia Cameron

Most Tarcher/Penguin books are available at special quantity discounts
for bulk purchase for sales promotions, premiums, fund-raising, and
educational needs. Special books or book excerpts also can be created
to fit specific needs. For details, write Penguin Group (USA) Inc.
Special Markets, 375 Hudson Street, New York, NY 10014.

Jeremy P. Tarcher/Penguin
a member of
Penguin Group (USA) Inc.
375 Hudson Street
New York, NY 10014
www.penguin.com

Library of Congress Cataloging-in-Publication Data

Cameron, Julia, date.
Answered prayers: love letters from the divine / Julia Cameron.
p. cm.
ISBN 1-58542-351-3
1. God—Attributes. 2. Affirmations. 3. Prayers. I. Title.
BL205.C35 2004 2004046041
204'.33—dc22

Printed in the United States of America
5 7 9 10 8 6 4

This book is printed on acid-free paper. ∞

BOOK DESIGN BY AMANDA DEWEY

Answered Prayers

Love Letters from
the Divine

JULIA CAMERON

JEREMY P. TARCHER/PENGUIN
a member of Penguin Group (USA) Inc.
New York

Preface

THE SMALL PRAYER BOOK that you hold in your hands is intended to work two ways. First, it identifies the spiritual issues that may be troubling you: loneliness, despair, boredom, financial insecurity, frustration, grief, uncertainty, and more. Second, it addresses those issues with the assurance that we are beloved exactly as we are. In this sense, the prayers are not only articulated but answered. Each page of this book raises a problem and moves to resolve it. Reading each prayer, we are asked to ascend from our human perspective to a divine perspective, from which our troubles may appear very different. What we perceive as our failings, God may view as opportunities for help and growth. What we may view as our all-too-human foibles, God may view as the very nature that he created and loves. The kindness of God may be for some of us a revelation.

While a book like this may be read in one sitting, it is perhaps wiser to proceed more thoughtfully, reading one prayer daily or perhaps a few, bearing in mind that some difficult topics will be addressed multiple times. Repetition in a book like this is a deliberate matter. We return to troublesome topics over and over again. Issues like financial insecurity are not often resolved with a single prayer. Rather, these are issues we bring to the altar of our heart again and again. We need to be reassured more than one time that all is well.

All is well. That is the message of this book. It is my hope that the language of this book will reach your heart.

Answered Prayers

YOU LONG FOR a more spiritual life, but you tell yourself that is too difficult. You pretend I am distant and hard to reach. You pretend I make harsh terms with you. Stop your pretending. Do not believe in God as told to you by the authorities. Come to me on your terms instead. Simply say "hello," and our conversation can begin.

I want to walk with you as friends walk. I want us to be casual and intimate. I want us to share secrets. I will begin with a secret of mine: I love you. I have loved you since the beginning of time. I have always seen myself as coming to join you. I am ready to listen to your heart. Please begin to talk with me. You can start anywhere, with your joys or with your sorrows. I have ears for every part of you.

You say you do not know where to begin. I say to you, "Quit stalling." Start with "good morning." And it is a good morning any day that you make contact with me. Ask me to shape your day, to touch your consciousness with the recognition of possibility. All things are good and can be made anew. I am the water you long to drink. I am the food you hunger for. I am the full meal that nourishes and nurtures you. Let us break bread.

YOU DO NOT feel worthy of knowing me. You are
not "spiritual," you say. Let us begin at the beginning.
No matter how you deny it, you are spiritual. That is your
true nature. You are a part of me and I am a part of you.

There is one power flowing through all of life, and we
are that power. As you open your mind to the fact that we
are already connected, our connection deepens. I am your
friend. I intend you nothing but good. As you open your
heart to the love in our connection, our bond strengthens.
You may be humble, yet you are spiritual in nature.

You do not need to become something you are not. I
love and accept you exactly as you are. It is easy to get to

know me. Begin as you would greet anyone, with a simple "hello." If you greet me and then listen, you will feel a response. This is how I speak to you; this is why they call it the still, small voice.

I speak gently and quietly but you can hear me. You can feel our connection. I do touch your soul. Do not worry about being worthy of knowing me. I am your maker and I make nothing that is not of the highest worth. I value you. I esteem you. I love you. Use my opinion to measure yourself. Come to me and feel your true nature.

LET'S BEGIN with your anxiety. Why are you frightened? Why do you believe I will not call for you? You are precious to me. I know every hair on your head. I hear your sighs. I watch over you while you are sleeping. You are my child.

Sophistication is difficult. You put me at a distance. You want to run your own life and then you wonder at its emptiness. Allow me to come close to you. Let me harbor your heart. You can tell me your fears. You can tell me your terrible imaginings. To begin with, you imagine you are alone. This is never true. When you wake up, I am there. My hands are ready to hold your day. Place your worries in my care. There is nothing too large or too small for me. I am ready to hold it all. I am waiting for you. I am patient.

It grieves me that you wake up frightened. I feel your fear and long to ease your pain. You are beloved. I do not care to see you suffer. Come to me. Bring me your problems. Ask me your questions. I have solutions for you. I hold answers. Nothing is too much for me. There is nothing too hard or too complex. Your difficulties are a source of joy for me as I untangle them. It delights me to be your aid. Come home to me. Pretend we are little children. Tell me your secrets. I have a listening heart.

You are shy with me. You feel awkward opening your heart. Go slowly, then. I will not go away. I am always present to you, near as your heartbeat, close as your breath. You can talk to me. I am waiting to hear what you will say. Begin gently. Tell me what I know. Say that you are lonely. I see this in you. I am with you always and yet you feel alone. Allow me to comfort you. Let me speak to your silent heart, saying that it is safe with me. I am your safety. Imagine that you are safe. Imagine that you can breathe freely, that I am your breath.

There is no darkness in which I cannot find you. My eye sees you always. You are accounted for. It troubles me that you feel invisible. You are always seen. You cannot come or go without my knowing your place. You belong with me. Ask me to be your companion. I am always near. As you walk, I walk with you. As you face your day, I face it too. I am ready to serve you. I am your servant and your guide. Let me help you to find your path. Let me walk with you one footfall at a time.

Do you remember how lovers speak? We can speak that softly. We can touch our open hearts. Reach for me and you will find me waiting. I am your friend.

WHAT IS this terror? Why does your breath catch in your throat? Why do you fear your future? I am with you always. There is nothing you must face alone. In the darkest night, I am there beside you. You sleep within my arms. I hold you cradled to my heart. Listen to what I say. It is all good. There is beauty everywhere. I bring joy. I bring comfort. I bring hope. And I bring it to all corners of this earth.

You are confused. This world is difficult. How can I allow it? you ask yourself. Freedom is beautiful, I answer. Mistakes may be made, but good always comes from evil. Invite me to help and then witness what I do. I am the great comforter. I bring solace. There is no pain I cannot assuage. There is a plan of goodness for everything. I am grace. I am the miraculous unfolding. Bring me your wounds. Allow me to relieve you. I am the nurse with healing hands. I am the balm that you are seeking. Bring me your troubled heart. Bring me your torment, your agony, your distress. I am ready to meet you.

Nothing is beyond my scope. No nightmare overwhelms me. In chaos and adversity, I see opportunity and hope. I am responsive to all suffering. I step forward in times of pain. Do not imagine you must go forward unaccompanied. Even unfelt, I am always there. You are cocooned.

YOU HAVE an anxious heart. Your fears overshadow your dreams. Your stories frighten you. You put me to one side, striving to act strong and brave, but your solitude undermines you. It is a lie. You are not alone. You are never unpartnered. I am here. I am with you always.

Bring me your anxious heart. Give me your terrors. I will protect your dreams. I know your dreams, for they are my children. Dreams come from God. God has the power to accomplish them. These are not idle words. I can bring you your dreams. Allow me to.

Tell me your sad stories. I see where you have been hurt again. Allow me to defend you. Allow me to shape your story. It can end well. Happiness does not elude me. I hold joy and expectation. I hold hope. Hope is an unmet friend, a source of strength.

You are afraid to hope. You tell yourself you are wise to be cautious, that caution serves your heart. Be brave with me instead. Allow me to risk while I protect your heart. I am large enough for you to be small. Picture this. There is a pocket above my heart. It is there that I carry you. You are safe. You are provided for. I act on your behalf as you allow me to act. Invite me to be your defender.

Your anxious heart seeks safety. I am the safety you seek. Come home to me. Allow my arms to give you shelter, give you peace.

YOU FALL ASLEEP frightened. This hurts my heart. I long to comfort you. I long to hold you steady in my arms, cradled serene and safe. I want you to fall asleep laughing, to sleep with a smile on your lips. I will guard you while you rest. I will protect you as you dream. You do not need to be vigilant. I am your protector. I cherish you.

The night holds no threat for me. I welcome its blackness and its calm. I planned the night. It is intended to comfort you. The stars watch over you as you sleep. The moon keeps an eye on you. You are not alone. You are well guarded.

Allow me to meet you at nightfall. Tell me your day before you sleep. Tell me the dreams you are harboring. Allow me to weave them while you rest. I am able to fulfill your dreams. I have miracles at my disposal. I am all powerful and, too, I am your friend. Come dream with me.

Rest in my arms. Confide your secrets to me. Tell me of each day's journey. I listen with a lover's heart. I am ready to hear all that you have to say. Nothing you whisper is too small for me. Nothing you sigh is too large for me. I am your perfect partner. I am the safety that you yearn for, the harbor you fear you cannot find. Of course you can find me. I am with you always. I am a part of you as you are a part of me. Can you see that we are one?

You miss those who have departed. Of course you do. They have your love. But love does not die, nor do lovers. Those who have left us are with us still. We are all one. There is one pure energy that unites us all. Feel our union, not our separation. Feel our communion and our grace. Open your heart to the more that awaits.

Those who have gone are with us still. We do not walk alone. Spirits advise us. Spirits comfort us. Spirits partner us on our journeys. To know this fact, we need only open our heart to it. Our loved ones are waiting, ready and eager for our touch. We open the gate to their presence. We invite their counsel and love. We are the ones who have slipped out of touch. They remember us. We are their beloveds and they love us still. Talk to them.

Do not be sorrowing and shy. Reach out in faith and allow connection to continue. Life is richer than we dream. Life is eternal. Life does not die. Our beloveds change their form but not their essence. They continue to hold us dear and to touch our lives.

All of life is alive to us. There are forces and forms beyond our imaginings that intend us good. Open your heart to higher forces. Allow life to move through you. Reach out to those who have moved on. Offer your love, your faith, your continued friendship. Receive the blessing intended for you from those who have stepped beyond.

OUR CITIES are not soulless. They are cathedrals. The high spires of man's endeavors reach toward God. Do not feel lost among the multitudes. My eye is always upon you. The crowded city street still is in my safekeeping. Each face is known to me. Each face is beloved.

You worry that your prayer goes unanswered. You worry that too many ask too much. I am an infinite energy. I do not tire. I am not overwhelmed. Your prayers are known to me. I hear your voice and listen as you speak. You are beloved. No other is like you. You cannot be replaced. I cherish your face, the slope of your shoulder, the grace of your hand. You are known to me amid all others. My only wish is that you draw near.

I made this earth to comfort you. The gentle willow, the soaring hawk, the tall grasses bending in the wind. All of these are your companions. The deer, the fox, the raven. These are your allies and your comrades who grace the earth. Amid concrete and steel, still remember my gifts to you. Amid crowds, remember that you are never alone. I am with you always. There is no step you take that I do not take with you. I ride with you on the crowded subways. I wait beside you for the bus. Closer than your shadow, I am your companion. In your city canyons, I am with you still and with you always, near as your breath.

You fear your future. Why? I will be there. I will lead you step-by-step as I lead you now—when you allow me.

Wake with me in the mornings. Place your days in my care. Allow me to shepherd you. Permit me to be your guide. I am with you always. Allow me to act on your behalf. The world is not too worldly for me. I have the skills to manage your affairs. Simply come to me. Bring me your problems and your goals. I have the power to move mountains. I can make straight your path.

Do not consider that your world revolves without me. This is mistaken and this causes grief both to you and to myself. Your world is my world. I am everywhere; in all things, in all exchanges, I am present. Tell me your needs. Open your heart to me. Let me shape your ways.

I did not set the world in motion and then leave it to its own devices. What parent would abandon its child? I watch every step with interest. I am always here to lend a steadying hand. Remember this: you are supported by my infinite love. I care for you. I see you as you strive. In me lies all potential, all possibility. It is my joy to expand through you. As you become what you wish to be, I, too, become what I wish to be. The future is our garden. We carry the seeds of our own unfolding. Allow me to be your sunshine, water, and rich soil. Plant your dreams in my care and allow me to nurture their growth. Your future is beautiful. Allow your heart to trust me.

TRUST MY BENEVOLENCE. Trust the goodness of my plan for you. You are unique. So, too, is my plan for your unfolding. I hold infinite possibilities. I hold surprise, joy, and exuberance. Your days are not a drudgery to be lived out with a hollow heart. Allow me to fill your days. Give your days to my care and let me walk with you. We walk in grace.

I have shaped your body. Its muscles and sinews are dear to me. I see your gentle strength. Your body is the body of God. I am within you always. Treat me with compassionate care. Allow me rest, water, calm walks to stir my limbs. Your body is my body. We are sacred. We are beautiful. We move in peace.

Do not be discouraged by your self-criticisms. Put judgment aside and feel my acceptance of all that you are. You are dear to me. I love all of you. Your fears are known to me. You can tell me your secret heart. I am safe for you. It is safe to trust your will and your life into my care. I am eager to help you.

There are no emergencies. Before you ask, I know your concerns. My goodwill precedes you. There is no situation too complex, no difficulty too extreme for me to handle. I am your safe harbor amid turbulent seas. Come to me. Allow me to shelter you. My intentions toward you are always kindly. Do not fear my guiding hand. I steer you always toward your highest good. There is no error in trusting my ways.

YOU ARE AFRAID to call on me. You doubt that I will answer. You fear you pray in vain. Call on me now. Offer me the chance to enter your heart. You have the key to the lock. Swing the door open through willingness. There, let me see your soul. Let me hear your whispering. I am here with you. Tell me your fears.

Why do you doubt my love? Have you sustained too many losses, more than your heart could bear? Bring to me your burdened heart. Speak to me of what your life has cost you. Tell me whom and what you miss. I am listening.

I will not tell you loss is trivial. I have known my own losses, many losses, and I know their pain. What I can promise you is that life will comfort life. More will come to you. More will fill your heart. In grief, the heart closes. We are afraid to love. We are afraid to extend ourselves, saying, "I have done that—and it hurt." Of course it hurt. I understand your wounds. I have had my own and, too, I carry yours as mine. And so I know this: we must open the grieving heart to love.

Bring me your battered heart. Allow me to comfort you. Walk with me a little ways. I will share your burden. I will carry your grief. As I open my love to you, do not resist me. Allow my heart to touch your heart. Unclench your heart for me. There. I will go softly, remembering the names of all you have lost, remembering your pain and your love.

You are lonely. Your heart is locked in fear. You cannot relax your vigilance. Your life is up to you. These are the thoughts that seize you upon awakening. You face your day numbly with a sense of dread. Allow me to change these things. Allow me to befriend you.

I am your constant companion. Greet me when you wake. I am beside you, facing all that you face in each day's march. You are not alone. I am with you as your ally. You do not walk alone. Give me your burdens. Let me carry the weight of your days. Follow me and feel your day's grace. I have people I wish you to meet, like-minded kindred spirits who will speak to your heart. Release your anxiety. Allow me to pave the way. Others are waiting to meet you. They yearn, as you do, for a common bond.

Life is an intricate dance, but you are never unpartnered. I am your partner and I contain multitudes. As you turn toward me, you turn toward your fellow man. I connect all of life. There is one mind, one energy, running through all creation. As you join me, you join the stars, the winds, the flowers. I am in all things. All things come to pass through me. Bring me your lonely heart and allow me to fill it with divine companions.

You ARE CONFUSED. Your way feels blocked. You do not know which way to turn. I am aware of how you feel. I sense your confusion. Allow me to remove your obstacles. Allow me to clear the way.

Your path lies within me. I can make straight your way. Do not try to journey on without me. Ask my help. Claim me as your guide. My way has clarity and integrity. My way brings you strength. In your confusion, turn to me and I will lead you. Ask to be guided, prompted, and led. You will sense my presence. You will feel my guiding hand.

There is no complication I cannot ease. There is no problem I cannot resolve. I am infinite wisdom, and as you open to me, I am active in your affairs. Allow me to untangle your heart. Invite my guidance and feel relief. Without me, life is too difficult. Without me, life is half dead. I grow trees from tiny acorns. I fill the fields with bountiful supply. In nature, my wisdom brings the seasons and so, too, I can harmonize your life. Let your confusion end in me. I will clear for you a way and a path. Stay close to me. I hold the lantern, dispelling your anxiety. I am your chosen path.

THERE IS NOT ENOUGH, you worry. How will you be cared for? There is enough. There is more than enough. There is plenty. This earth is abundantly blessed. I am aware of your needs and I provide for them. It is my pleasure to fulfill your needs. My supply underlies all things. Whether it is food you have need of, or money, turn to me. Turn to me always. I am always here. I am the storehouse of your good.

The earth does not run without me. I am present at all times, in all ways. Invite me to enter your business affairs. Invite me to prosper you. It is my pleasure. I am an expansive energy. Allow me to expand through you, invite me to become more large. I am the great giver. Allow me to gift you. It is my nature to give and yours to receive. Accept this law. I am waiting to serve you. I hold all that you require.

For every thought of need, there is a gift of supply. Bring me your empty cup that I can fill it. Bring me your plate that I can heap it high. God has no empty coffers. I am filled to overflowing with your good. You need only come to me. You need only ask that you can receive. Believe that I am your source. Affirm that and be prospered.

YOU HAVE MADE a mistake and fear that there is no undoing it. I am glad to know your thoughts, but I have news for you. It is never too late to turn to me. There is no error I cannot undo. Come to me now. That is sufficient.

I am all powerful. Miracles are commonplace for me. I deal with them daily. I mend the broken bonds of love. I heal the shattered households. I guide the safe return of love. Allow me to handle your mangled affairs. Stick close to me. Do as I guide you to do. Behind your smallest act is the infinite strength of the universe. Allow me to act through you. Give me your heart that I may teach it to love.

There is no distance too great for me. There is no rift too large. I am the great healer. All souls respond to me. There is no one too hardened to feel my touch. Bring me your difficulties. Invite me to solve them. Tell me the error of your ways. I hear your heart. I know you long for healing. You do well to come to me. I am the dear and glorious physician. Nothing is too broken for my repair. Where there is life, there is hope, and I am life itself. Live within me now. Live with a quiet expectation of good. Nothing is too damaged to be fixed by me. Bring me your broken dreams.

You do not trust yourself to pray rightly. But there is no prayer I cannot hear. I know your voice. I know it as a shout or a whisper. I know it as a sigh or a moan. Any prayer is a prayer that reaches me. I am always listening for you.

How many times can I assure you? You are beloved to me. There is only one of you and you're my precious child. From the beginning of time, I waited for you to take your place. Your smallest prayer looms large to me. I do not set difficult terms. Call me by any name that serves you. I am father, mother, creator, and your Lord. Any name will get my attention. You have my attention before you call.

In a small voice, ask me to care for you. It is my pleasure. Shout aloud the dreams you would have me fulfill. Your shouts, like your whispers, are mine to attend to. I hear you loud or soft. I hear you loud and clear.

There are times when you pray with difficulty, when your prayers are nothing more than yearnings. I hear those too. You are my creature. Your ways are known to me. I am attentive. You are in my care. Prayer reminds you, more than it does me, of our loving relationship. I love you always. I listen before you speak. You cannot pray a prayer I cannot hear. There is no wrong way to reach out to me. Pray as it serves you to pray. Choose your prayers like flowers gathered from a field. Each prayer is dear to me. Each prayer is heard. A clover, a lily, a rose, a sunflower, a zinnia, an aster—each is perfect in its own way, as are your prayers.

YOUR LIFE FEELS overwhelming. Your future looms large and unknown. Turn to me. Let me be a source of comfort. Ask me for help so that your agitation and stress may be lifted. Allow me to shoulder your burdens.

The future unfolds one day at a time. Respect that pace. Do not hurry forward into tomorrow. Allow me to lead you, to enter your days and fill them with peace. I have a peaceful heart for you. Enter my heart and allow me to share my abundant sense of well-being. Unfold your days with me and lose your sense of panic and loss. This earth is abundant. It holds joy for you, and contentment. Bring me your restless heart. Allow me to gentle your soul. When you go forward without me, there is always a sense of grasping. You fear there is not enough to fill your hungry heart.

Walk with me and discover bounty. There is more than enough to fill your heart. Take time with me. Allow me to set the pacing of your day. Relax with me. Allow me to grace your days with quiet productivity. There is no rush. The present well spent builds the future. Each day is a gift to you. Each day contains time enough for harmony. Give me your sense of urgency. Allow me to transform it into a sense of purpose. Give me each day and I will give it back to you transformed and shining with love.

SIMPLICITY IS threatening. But simplicity is useful because it reflects the truth: there is one power, one source, upholding all of life. Depending on that power is a dependency on reality, the great reality that is all that is. And so I say to you, depend on me. Trust me and turn to me in all things. Nothing is too complex for my understanding. Nothing is too difficult for my simple care. I am the source.

My will for you is goodness. You can trust me to unfold your world. Bring me those areas that trouble you. Ask my guidance and I will give you direction. I am willing and able to solve your life's problems. You are my creation, and your comfort is my concern. I have given you your very nature. You can trust me to shape your world.

There is no area of your experience of which I am ignorant. I am the source of all. I see your needs for companionship, for rewarding work, for a safe and lovely dwelling place. I understand your desire for an abundant flow and for security. Allow me to establish you on my footing. Trust me to provide for you. It is my joy.

You HAVE the right to my help. I am your creator. Your problems are my problems. Ask me for help. I give it to you gladly. I am saddened when you try to live alone. My desire for you is union and fulfillment. I am your answered prayer. I am always what you seek.

You are a part of me. We are one energy and one mind. As you ask me to help in your affairs, I am able to enter your life. All that is required of you is your willingness to rely upon me. Trust me to prosper you. My goal for you is expansion and abundance. As you turn to me with your desires, I have the power to fulfill them. Rely on me totally. Trust me to put in place a grid of right opportunities. Trust me to lead you, carefully and gently, one step at a time into your good.

Your well-being is my concern. I desire your happiness. Allow me to aid you in every undertaking. Bring me your wishes and your hopes. Open your heart to me and dare to be specific. I see you as unique and particular. Allow me to help you in concrete and individualized ways.

YOU HAVE A restless heart. You do not trust your life's unfolding. You look for trouble and, in quiet times, you manufacture difficulty. You are addicted to anxiety. I offer you calm and you turn me aside. Now I ask you: quiet your heart for me. Allow me to enter your life as a soft wind bringing freshening change. It is possible to change gently. It is possible to grow without drama. I offer you that chance. Accept my gardening hand.

When you are restless, turn to me. Ask me to take away your agitation and direct your thinking along positive lines. You can learn to live peacefully. You can learn that I am ever present to calm your fears. Let your thoughts of me become habitual. Learn to remember I am at your side, ready always to dismantle your difficulties. There is no vexation that I cannot help you with. The situations of your life are familiar to me, and I can bring my grace to bear.

Allow me to calm your heart. Trust me now with your life's unfolding. Do not look for trouble. Do not manufacture problems. Accept my calm and come willingly to my shelter. In me, your restless heart finds a quiet abode. I am the calm center from which all things are possible. Allow me to nurture your growth.

YOU ANTICIPATE DANGER, dreading the worst. Your imagination dwells in the negative, frightening your heart. Allow me to change your perspective. Join me in seeing good, not evil. Take optimism as a daily path.

I am optimistic. In all things, I see potential for good. There is no difficulty that cannot be eased. There is no wound that cannot heal. Life is resilient. You are a part of life, and therefore you, too, are resilient. Call on your strength. Call on your power. Call on your grace. You are a part of me and I am a divine energy. I am all-powerful. Therefore so are you. You have only to call on me. I answer when you call.

When you turn to me, I am there, waiting for you. It is my pleasure to serve you, my pleasure to bring you good. Turn your heart toward the positive. Learn to see good in all things. Anticipate safety, not danger. Anticipate success, not failure. Anticipate fulfillment, not disappointment. Let your imagination dwell on the good, comforting your heart. It is possible to attain this perspective. Optimism is a practiced choice.

Join me in my optimism. See the potential for good in everything. Know your own resilience. Claim your own heritage. You are strong, powerful, and graceful. There is one mind, one spirit, running through all of life. Trust this sacred source of all goodness. Allow it to be your guide.

YOU FEEL yourself separate. You fear yourself small. You see the world as large and threatening. I tell you, you are wrong. You are a part of me and I am very large. You are as large as you need to be to face your problems. You are larger than you know. Name your problem and bring it to me. Already, it is smaller. I am larger than your cares, larger than your woes. I am almighty, infinite, all reaching. Nothing that you bring to me overwhelms me.

It is all a matter of perspective. To me, you are large and your problems are small. You are what I am focused upon. You are the point of my loving concern. I am an infinite power. I have all the strength, all the wisdom, all the grace you need. Nothing you bring to me is too much for me. It gives me joy to grapple with your difficulties. I delight in solving your problems. Your difficulties are my toys. It is child's play for me to untangle your life. I take pleasure in helping you.

For me, you are never separate, never small. I made this world as my gift to you. It is my joy when you enjoy it, when you feel safe and secure. This is my intention for you always. Take comfort in me as your creator and your protector. You are my own.

You are afraid of being poor. You focus on what you will lack. To you, the future feels uncertain. This is false thinking. I am the source of your good. My resources are infinite. My flow is abundant. My wealth is real. Depend on me for your well-being. Your future good is certain with me.

All of life is one energy, ever expanding, ever becoming more. You are a part of this energy, and it is my pleasure to expand you and give you more. I am the great giver, ever more prosperous, ever more generous. I am ever an increase in all things. For me to partner you, you must learn to receive. Expect my bounty to flow to you. Feel gratitude in your heart that this is so. Bring me your grateful heart as a cup that I can fill to overflowing. Expect me to further your good.

I am the source of all things. No human power can subvert my flow. At all times, in all places, my good can reach you. My goodness to you cannot be blocked, so why do you fear? Affirm daily, "God is my source." Boldly claim the abundance of God as your right and reward. It is my great joy to bring you fulfillment. Your wishes and desires draw me to you. Ask and you shall receive. I am your source.

YOU ARE BORED and discontented. Your life feels shallow. You forget I answer dreams. When you are bored and discontented, it is because you have closed me out. You have forgotten that I am the source of all things, including people and adventures. Ask me to bring you what you need. It is my pleasure to introduce you to richer life. I know the people you should meet, the adventures you should have. Give me your life and allow me to enrich it in every way.

When you say your life is shallow, you are forgetting my depths. Come to me for deeper meaning. Come to me for your soul's sense of adventure. I am the one power running through all of life. I contain everything. Nothing is beyond my grasp. Bring me your discontent. Bring me your boredom. Allow me to make your shallow life deep. Allow me to answer your dreams.

Take a hold of me. Embrace me. Hold me to your heart. As you give yourself wholeheartedly to me, I am able to give back to you with greater abundance. Do not be a miser with your spirit. Commit to me. Spend energy on me and I will reward you with a life beyond your dreams.

YOU ARE AFRAID to commit. You cling to half measures. You blame me for your life but refuse to allow me to alter it. Bring me your whole heart. Open your life to me without reservation. Allow me the freedom to act on your behalf. I am the source of your good. Allow me to flow freely into your life. Give me all of you. Allow me to act in all areas of your life. There is no arena in which I cannot bring change for the better.

I am an energy of improvement. At all times, in all places, I work to bring about an improvement of conditions. Allow me to perfect your life. Ask that every cranny and nook of your experience be brought into alignment with my will for you. Seek to know my will for you and to cooperate with that will's unfolding. I promise you the betterment of your life.

As you commit to me, you commit also to yourself, to your highest good. There is no contradiction between my desires for you and your own highest good. Seek to know yourself in me. Allow me to expand your thinking and enlarge your scope of action. I have a large plan for you. I am completely committed to your well-being. As you align your will with mine, your life is made whole and perfect. Commit to your highest destiny and allow me to act. Give me your all.

You DOUBT your originality. You doubt the validity of your ideas. This is false thinking. In all of time, there is only one of you. You are a unique expression of the divine mind. Divine mind thinks through you. Your ideas come from God and God has the power to accomplish them. Put your faith in this.

Because there is one divine mind, our ideas are divine in origin. They are potent and original. They draw their potency and originality from a divine source. That divine source knows how to prosper them. As we turn to the creator to manifest our creativity, we are gently and carefully led. A step at a time, we are given to know our proper unfolding. Divine mind sees no obstacles, only opportunities. Divine mind connects those who should be connected for their highest good. There is no place for compromise, no place for disappointment. The divine mind thinks through all of us. All of us, in turn, think through the divine mind. As we ask to be prospered and led, we are prospered and led. Divine mind seeks always the betterment of all in all things.

Do not doubt your originality. Do not doubt the validity of your ideas. Claim instead your birthright as a cocreator inspired with divine energy, filled with divine ideas. Know that, at all times, divine mind is behind you and your thinking. It is God's will for you to succeed.

YOU FEAR LACK. You doubt your share in God's abundance. Take a moment now and affirm that you are a part of divine abundance. It is God's will to prosper you. It is God's pleasure to give you the kingdom.

Behind every idea of need, there is the reality of divine supply. God has more than enough of whatever it is you require—a house to live in, rewarding work to do, a happy and affirmative relationship. Take your needs directly to God. Ask that your needs be fulfilled from the divine abundance. Know that it brings me pleasure to fulfill your needs. I am a giver. It falls to you to receive my gifts.

Accepting supply from the divine storehouse is not selfish. It demonstrates to others the practicality of dependence on God. Whatever you need, whenever you need it, God has a means to supply. God is a flowing-out of abundance, a flowing-out of love. Take time to reaffirm your unity with all of life. See through apparent stagnation and delay to the great reality taking on substance at your request. Living spirit prospers everything you do and everyone you meet. Every good increases. Success comes to you and to those you meet. The divine source will never fail us if we have faith in it. God has already made us the gift of abundance. Our good is there for the taking, like apples ripe on the tree. Accept God's prosperity as your own. Celebrate abundant life.

You have a sense of emergency. You doubt divine timing. You fear that my delay may be my denial. You do not trust me with your unfolding. Take a moment to consider the natural world. Think of the seasons and the magnificent way growth is orchestrated to occur exactly when and how it should. Place yourself in my gardening hands. Allow me to time your unfolding. Trust me with the seasons of your life—budding spring, blooming summer, the harvest time of fall, the quietude of winter.

Allow me to teach you when patience is in order and when it is a time for legitimate urgency. I have wisdom regarding cycles of growth and dormancy. I have wisdom regarding the proper nutrients for health. In divine order, all unfolds as it should unfold without haste and without waste. I am efficient. I make maximum use of the stores you entrust to me. Become a part of my garden. Become the seed that I nurture to full and glorious bloom. There is no emergency. My divine timing is perfect and serves you well. Trust my sense of right action. Your successful unfolding is my great joy.

You feel inadequate to face your life. You fear you lack inner resources. You consider yourself "not enough." This is false thinking. You are a child of the divine mind. Everything necessary for your successful life is a part of you now. You are more than enough. Place your dependency on me. This is not weakness. This is strength. Place your life in my careful hands. When you feel small, rely on me to be large. When you feel "not enough," rely on me to be more than enough.

I am divine mind. I know how to meet every circumstance with calm. No situation is too difficult for me to handle. I am ready to meet all possibilities and handle them with grace.

Do not feel inadequate to face your life. You are designed to face life, but not alone. You are intended to be a part of me. Allow me to go before you and prepare the way. Reliance upon me does not diminish you. Reliance upon me makes you strong. Do not fear your lack of inner resources. I am your inner resource and I am infinite. When the outer world feels harsh, turn to your inner world and place your problems and predicament in my hands. It is my pleasure to bring you a fulfilling life.

YOU FEEL FATIGUED. You doubt your strength. Put aside such anxieties. Count on me for your resilience. Come to me for your strength.

I am the one mind. All things are made from me. Your body is fashioned from my energy. My energy sustains its health. Come to me for greater well-being. Come to me as infinite source. Do not rely on your own limited resources. Rely instead on my infinite fund of energy. Allow me to restore you. Allow me to bring you vital energy. I am your stamina. I am your strength.

Do not feel fatigued. Rest in me. Allow me to work through you. Allow me to perform whatever task feels difficult for you. I am boundless energy. I flow outward to you and I am available for your use. Think of me as spiritual electricity, a unique power that flows just where it is needed. Trust my energy to flow through you now. Ask to be a channel for my power and grace. Open yourself to me. Give me your heart and your mind. Give me your will and your life. As you give yourself to me, I give myself to you. All your prayers are answered prayers as I come to you, ready to meet your every need. Trust me as your divine source. My energy is yours to use.

YOU HAVE a sense of weariness. The world tires you. You hunger for renewal but seek to find it in sleep, not experience. You are too much with yourself. Come to me. Let me wake you gently. Let me show you the world through my eyes. I have seen everything, and I have seen it over and over, but I am not tired of this world. To me, all things are new, all things are possible. You are not old. You are just being born. Your consciousness is just waking up to its potential.

Live with me. Commit to this life. It is an unfolding odyssey. You do not know the end of your journey. Each day holds new thoughts and new footfalls. Dare to have an adventurous heart. I do. I am the great adventure and I am available to you. Bring me your stagnant days and allow me to infuse them with freshness, with the flow of grace and ideas. I am brimming with life. I am a fountain of new thoughts and new experiences. Allow me to rejuvenate you. Bring me your tired soul. I am the deep water your spirit craves. I am the well you long to drink from to slake your travel-weary thirst. Come to me tired and worn. Ask me to refresh your heart. Offer me your long day's journey. We are only starting, you and I.

You ARE LONELY. You feel yourself isolated and friendless as you carry the burden of your life. Come to me. Let me be your colleague. Let me bear witness to your difficulties and your grace. I am eager to hear your story. I want to hear your heart's woes. You cannot tire me. You do not wear me out. You are beloved. In all your moods, in your times of sorrow and despair, you are dear to me.

Bring me your self-pity. I will gift you with humor. In shared laughter you will find your burden eased. I smile at your approach. Your perspective is unique to me and I value your candor. So you find the world a terrible place.

Let me comfort you. Let me hear your grief. If you talk to me, you will no longer be alone. I can befriend you. I can share with you your issues and privations.

Do not shun me. Do not pull yourself up and insist you be alone. I long to ease your suffering. I yearn to lessen your pain. I am the great nurturer. It brings me joy to give you solace. It delights me to hear you laugh. So many times our despair is caused by our alienation. We try to bravely go forward alone, little realizing we are not intended to be alone. Allow me to be your companion. Allow me to share your journey, to bear your burden, to heal your pain. You are my chosen friend. Let me love you.

You would like to avoid me. You are sad and you fear that contact with me will make you sadder still. "Let me be shallow," you say, but I must refuse you. Do not avoid me. I am not the cause of your pain. I am a witness to your life, but I do not bring grief with me. Sometimes grief lies simply in seeing what is. When you do that, you can turn to me. I will see what you saw. I will witness your sorrow.

I am the great comforter. I bring you solace, understanding, and hope. In times of despair, hope is what you have abandoned. You have said, "Do not ask me to care again." But you do care, and despite yourself you do need reassurance. Let me reassure you. Let me promise you there is more good to come.

Your life is not over, nor is your happiness. You will love again. Bring me your weary heart. Allow me to feel the depth of your melancholy. Do not hide from me your cynicism and the fact that all seems ashes. I can absorb your loss. I can withstand your pain. I am larger than the passing moment, larger even than the great losses you sustain. I am your comfort. I know how to gentle your savage heart. Bring me your wildness and your grief.

YOU HAVE lived enough. You are ready to quit if I will allow it. Your heart is tired and you would like to rest. I understand your fatigue. You have reached the end of your resources. Come to me. Let me bear your burdens. Let me do the work of your days. I am an infinite energy. I can carry you, and it is my pleasure to lessen your load. Although you may not acknowledge it, we are intimates, you and I. I know your aches and pains. I see your exertions.

In me, find your refreshment. In me, find your ease. Rest in me and refresh yourself. Let your fatigue slip away. My resources are yours now. You are plentifully supplied.

I have strength enough, stamina enough, and wisdom enough to shoulder all you have undertaken. Allow me to work through you. Open your heart that I may enter your life, touching all that you have touched. Allow yourself to be a hollow reed that I may breathe through you into your creations. Trust me now to take over your life's work and bring it to successful fruition.

YOU ARE A STORY with no listener. You are lonely, longing to share your tale. Pay attention to what I say. I am the great listener. I long to hear your thoughts and feelings. I am hungry to hear your heart. Bring me the small stories you have noticed. Bring me the grand adventures you have endured. Your life is the story I like best. Share your life with me.

Allow me to be your witness. Allow me to be your listening ear. Do not censor what you tell me. Bring me everything. I am hungry for it all. I love the stories that you tell. You surprise and delight me. Your actions fascinate me. You are the focus of my heart, my favorite story unfolding.

Do not be afraid that you bore me. I made you. Nothing about you is boring to me. Do not be afraid you tire me. I am tireless and always ready to listen. Find your voice. Clear your throat and speak to me easily. I am enchanted by you and all that you tell. Your words are more precious to me than any coins. Your thoughts are more valued than any jewels. Tell me your story. Unspool for me your lovely heart.

You HUNGER to be touched, but you deny your hunger. Allow me to love you. Permit me to teach you loving ways to treat yourself. Every hair on your head is precious to me, every inch of your skin. You are not a beast of burden. I do not intend you to work yourself to exhaustion, calling it virtue. Rest in me, my little one. Allow me to brush out your hair, to knead the sore muscles of your back. I am tender to you. Eat, sleep, refresh yourself.

When you regard your body, do so with tenderness. You are beautiful to me. You are unique and priceless. Learn to praise the beauties of your form. I have made you sturdy. I have given you health and strength. Your body is graceful to me. I am able to love an endless myriad of shapes and sizes. Do not turn a cruel eye to your body. It is the beloved vehicle for your spirit. It carries you faithfully.

Let me teach you to love yourself. Let me bathe and clothe you. You are a divine child. I find beauty in you always. It is my pleasure that you have comfort. It is my pleasure that you use your senses. I created your body for your enjoyment. Your sense of touch is sacred. Do not be cold and loveless, calling that grace. Warmth and compassion are my gifts to you. Relax and enjoy the gift of your body.

You PRAY for guidance and then doubt that I answer your prayers. I am always listening, always ready to guide you when you will be led. My voice speaks in a thousand forms. I may guide you through people or events. I may guide you through a quiet inner knowing. When you ask to be led, I hear your prayer and I send messengers. Be alert to my guiding hand. It is gentle and always present. You are never lost to me. I am always in conscious contact with your spirit.

Pray to me for guidance and then trust your inner promptings. I speak to you through intuition: the hunch, the inkling, the urge. I guide you lightly, and I always leave your own will intact. You are free to ask for guidance or not. You are free to follow my guidance or not. Your freedom is important to me. I do not coerce you to my ways.

The world can be a loud and busy place. Seek quiet and calm and you will more easily find me, although I am always there amid the tumult and the hubbub as well. To find me, you need only to seek me. The smallest prayer is enough for me to hear. If you pray constantly, we can enjoy a conversation. It is my pleasure to speak to you.

You CALL ON ME, then hurry onward, not waiting for a response. You feel a duty to be busy always. You rush through your days. Relax and take it easy. Allow me to set the pacing of your day. I can move with great velocity when it is necessary, but so much rush and hurry are not necessary.

I am a master of timing. Consider the planets in their course. Consider, too, the seasons. You surely can see the wisdom in these. Your life, too, can be timed to a fruitful unfolding. Come to me and ripen within my love. Allow me to shelter you. Allow me to provide you with safety.

Stay close to me and allow me to cue your actions. There is no emergency.

You rush to cover your anxiety. Instead, bring your anxious heart to me. Allow me to calm your fears. Place your hasty ways in my care. Allow me to create your path. There is time enough for all good things.

You look to the future with fear. Allow me to deliver you. As I give you knowledge of your next step, take that step. Know that each step is calmly linked into a great, unfolding plan. My plan has time enough that hurry has no place in it. Quiet your hectic heart. Allow me to speak to you gently. Listen and hear the heartbeat of your unfolding. It is as graceful and certain as the grass.

YOU FEEL DEPRESSED. The weight of the world is too much for you. The very thought of it makes you sigh. Come to me. Bring me your fatigue and your sorrow. I am an infinite energy. You cannot tire me, wear me out, or use me up. Share with me your doubt and your despair. I am your renewal. I am your source of optimism and strength. I can lift your heart.

This earth is my gift to you. Its million beauties are to be a solace to you. Consider the glory of the setting sun. Enjoy the moonrise. Daily I bring the breeze to freshen your spirit. I bring birdsong and the scent of flowers. In all these things, in all these ways, I comfort you. I have made you a sensitive creature. Your moods are like weather. When they trouble you, come to me. Allow me to be your weather. Enjoy the sunshine of my companionship. Bask in the gentle breeze of my understanding.

Your depression is exhaustion. Like Atlas, you try to carry this world on your own shoulders. This was never my intention. Allow me to carry the world. I invented it, after all. Your only job is to walk with me as my companion and my friend. Allow me to cheer you on your way. Allow me to offer you hope and comfort. Allow me to heal your despair.

You are frightened and feel yourself unbalanced. You dread the future and doubt your capacity to face it. Calm yourself. Today is the day we must deal with, and for today I can be your strength. Rely on me. Allow me to ease your fears. Permit me to bring you balance. As the future unfolds, I will be your unshakable ally and friend. There is nothing you must face alone. I am with you always. I am your fortress, your harbor, your home. In me lies all protection. Come to me.

When you are frightened, it is because you have put distance between us. When you dread the future, it is because you forget my care. You are not alone. You are a part of me and I am all safety, all calm, all grace. When you are carried in my heart, what can harm you? You have no enemies when you rely on me.

I am the great harmonizer. I bring peace and resolution to all discord. I bring the successful working-out of all problems. Bring to me the knotted skein of your life. I can untangle your affairs. I can weave for you a new and beautiful tapestry. It is my pleasure to serve you in this way. I bring beauty to all I touch. Allow me to touch your life, to contain your future in my care. All is well with me and well with you. Only come to me.

You ARE AFRAID of poverty. You do not trust your supply to sustain itself. Looking to the future, you project lack, not abundance. You fear I am capricious, here today and gone tomorrow, leaving you alone and destitute. What terrible imaginings! How counter to my true nature.

I am abundance itself. It is my great joy to provide for you. Wherever you have need, I have supply. It is my nature to fulfill your wants. It is my nature to be steadfast and generous. I am the great provider. Come to me with your cup half-empty and allow me to fill it. Allow me to help you husband your resources. I am an expansive energy. It is my delight to expand your life. Rely on me for the flow of goodness that comes to you. I am not merely abundant. I am infinite. You cannot exhaust my reserves. You cannot require too much of me.

As you have need, so shall I give to you. It is not my desire for you to count pennies, hoarding your resources against hard times. Instead, trust me to buffer hard times. Trust that my substantial flow is dependable and steady. Build your life on my outflow. What I have I give to you, and I have more than enough, always, to sustain your needs. Do not fear financial insecurity. Cherish what you hold and expect it to be increased as you care for it. My abundance is your steady source.

You doubt that you are lovable. When you look to your future, you see yourself alone, old, and foolish. These thoughts are demons, nothing more. You are lovable. Even as we speak, you are greatly beloved. I cherish you. To me you are more valuable than diamonds, emeralds, sapphires, or rubies. You are my great treasure, the pearl beyond price. If I love you, and I do, why would I plan for you a life that is joyless and loveless?

It is my pleasure to bring you love. It is my joy to fill your heart. Trust me to find a match for you. Allow me to work on your behalf. In all the world, there is no one else quite like you. You are unique and irreplaceable. Allow me to bring you love. Let me choose for you one who can cherish you, one who can see your originality and honor it.

Your world is teeming with wonderful souls. Let me bring you to the attention of those who can see you clearly. Allow me to forge a network for you, introducing you to kindred spirits and to one special soul among them who fills your heart with joy and understanding. You are lovable. It is not your destiny to be alone, old, and foolish. Allow me to choose for you. Allow me to bring you companions worthy of your love.

You worry that your originality is flagging. You fear your ideas are stale or unworkable. You are afraid your time has passed. Make me your origin. I am a bottomless well of inspiration. I invite you to dip in.

I am the great thinker. With me as your source, your ideas are fresh and usable. You are in your prime. You are at the height of your creative endowment. Do not seek to separate yourself from me to be independent. Rather, rely on me. Lean on me. Depend on me. Let your glory come from reliance and not defiance. Open your mind to me. Present to me your puzzles and the areas in which you seek inspiration. Allow divine mind to enter human mind. Permit me to act through you.

As my thought is inspired, so, too, is yours. The originality of your ideas is beyond question. Your thought reflects my flexibility and innovation. Your thought reflects the power of my vision. Ask me to be your muse. Rely upon me to be your wellspring. Gently set all ego aside and be a channel for my thinking to come into the world. Trust that I think through you.

Your relationship feels broken. You are afraid all is lost. You despair of repairing it. You are on rocky times. Remember, I am the great lover. I am the one who makes all things anew. Allow me to mend your heart's folly. Permit me to act in your affairs. There is no rift too terrible for me to repair. There is no distance too great to be closed. My love heals all differences. My love restores harmony and balance.

Reach out to me with your broken heart. Tell me your disappointments, your hopes, and your dreams. Be vulnerable to me. Do not hide your heart from me.

I am, as I have told you, the dear and glorious physician. I can restore health to mangled relations. I can cure the woes of discouragement, the pains of loss. Allow me to reach you. Permit me to guide and counsel you. Acting through me, you act with wisdom and prudence. Acting through me, your good intentions are understood. I will give you words to say, actions to be taken. As you stay close to me and disclose your heart, I can fill your heart until it is brimming with love. Your full heart draws to itself a selfless love. Your goodwill meets with goodwill. Your love meets with love.

Your animal companions are needy. They, too, require my love. I am the creator of every life form: the kitten, the puppy, the bird, the bee. All creatures have their origin in me. All creatures are hungry for my touch. Come to me and tell me of those creatures you are husbanding. Ask for my guidance in their care.

There is no difficulty with which I am not familiar. There is no weakness or damage I have not foreseen. Trust your creatures to my care. Your pets are beloved to me also. Ask me to safeguard their health. Ask me to fathom their psyches. Ask me to search out their delight.

As you come to me for guidance, I will guide you. As you ask me for wisdom, I will make you wise. I will tutor your heart in how best to care for my creations. I will help you to comfort them and to bring them joy. In the devotion of your pets to you, I show you a small part of my devotion to your heart. Let us delight together in the animal kingdom. Let us rejoice together in its lovability. I offer you a boundless love to bestow on those creatures in your care. Those creatures in your care offer in return my boundless love to you.

YOUR HEALTH concerns you. You feel yourself weak and failing. Come to me. I am the source of your good health. I am the maker of all. I know precisely how to sustain your life force. Come to me with your questions and fears. Allow me to bring you radiant health and well-being. Allow me to bring you vitality.

There is one universal energy moving through all of life. I am that energy. Seek me out. I am the great healer, known to the ages as the dear and glorious physician. Come close to me. Offer me your body. Allow me to make it whole and perfect. I work through many means, through doctors and surgeons who will tell you that it is the action of something beyond them that heals. I am that something beyond.

When you seek your health, you are seeking me. I am whole. I am perfect. I am harmonious. Your radiant well-being is my delight. Seek guidance from me and I will lead you to healers who treat the body as a temple of the sacred. Seek guidance from me and I will lead you to right healings, a restoration of the health that is your birthright, an endowment from me, the source of all well-being. Come to me seeking your health. It is a wealth I gladly share with you.

YOU ARE FATIGUED. You have pushed your body beyond its limits. Your mind is tired and your spirit weak. Come to me. I am the rest and refreshment you are seeking. I am the running brook that soothes your soul. I am the black sky spangled with stars under which you can sleep. I am the great restorer.

Bring me your fatigue. Allow me to refresh you with food and comfort. Your tired body is my tender child, and I attend to it. Your stressed spirit calls for my healing touch. I answer gladly. It is my great pleasure to comfort you. Your weakness is my strength. Open your heart to me and allow me to sustain you.

I am without fatigue. I am without exhaustion. I gladly share with you from my storehouse of stockpiled energy. My vitality is your vitality. My radiant health is your health. Depend on me. As a loving parent leads a child with a tender hand, so will I lead you. One step at a time, never too quickly or with haste, I will bring you where you need to go. You are exhausted from trying to reach your objectives without me. Do not strive to be without me. Depend on me in all things. Allow your heart to be carried within my greater heart. Allow yourself to rest in my gentle custody. You are my beloved child. I cherish you.

Y<small>OUR HEART</small> is panicked. You imagine you are lost. Be still. Let me come to you. There is no darkness in which I cannot find you. You are known to me.

Gently tell your heart its panic is misplaced. There is no danger. There is no emergency. Where I am present, help is always at hand. Near as your breath—even nearer. Before you can gasp, "Help me," I hear and answer your prayer. Of course I will help you. You are my beloved child. Your terrors seize my heart. I long to comfort you. "There, there," I will say to you. "Rest in me. Rest. Rest."

I can always hear your prayer, however small, however terrified. In the choir of this world's voices, I know your voice. Speak to me. Tell me of your fears. Allow me to comfort you. Allow me to bring you peace.

I am always with you, always near. The only anxiety is my imagined absence. I am never absent. I am present for you always. There is no catastrophe, no loss you can sustain that could remove me from your side. I am always here for you, always ready to be your aid, your comfort, your ally. Mine is a peaceful world. Join me here.

You TURN a blind eye on the beauty that surrounds you. You are focused on harsh, unpleasant things. You call your focus realism. You cling to it like a barnacle to a rock. Listen to me. Allow my voice to reach your stubborn ears.

This earth is beautiful. There is at least as much beauty and generosity as selfishness and hatred. What you call realism is pessimism. You refuse to see the good. Of course you do. You have a broken heart. Bring it to me. Let me heal its anguish. You are afraid to hope. You have been hurt and disappointed in the past. You do not trust me. You do not trust the good.

Come near me. Let me speak to you plainly. It is true. Terrible things happen. Horrible events come to pass, but they are not my fault. I have gifted mankind with freedom. Sometimes that freedom is abused. This grieves me as it grieves you, but it is not, by far, the whole story. Every day, everyplace I look, goodness is afoot. It comes to the cities, where it may appear as a smile among strangers, the kindly offer of unexpected help. It comes to the country and villages, where neighbors seek to assist one another through hard times. Kindness is always just as visible as the cruelty you choose to see. Your eye does the beholding. I say to you, this is a beautiful world. Choose to see it so.

You do not think you can believe in me. You consider faith to be childish. You strive to be adult. By "adult," you mean lonely and disillusioned. Come to me. If you have not lost your capacity for awe, I can heal you.

Consider the natural world. A tiny disturbance creates the pearl in the oyster. Allow the disturbances of this world to create for you the pearl of faith. Great beauty can be born of chaos. Tragedy can call forward heroism in human hearts. Dare to see the good born of evil. Be disillusioned by your disillusionment. To be adult is to see further than the immediate. Lift up your eyes from catastrophe. What good is being born?

I am a limitless good. I pour into everything at all times and all places. I am the sustainer of life. I am the original source, the cause of all that you behold. If you have difficulties with my creation, bring those difficulties to me. Allow me to place in you sufficient understanding that your soul matures. It is childish to hold a grudge against me, childish to refuse to speak your mind. Join me in dialogue. Let me hear your tortured heart. You are not alone in finding me flawed. I see your discontent and I am ready to meet with you. Let us be adults. Talk to me.

YOU ARE high-strung and nervous. This world is too much with you. You long for peace. Come to me. I am the provider of peace. In me your nervousness can find a place of rest. I am steadfast and dependable. In a hectic world, you can count on me. Bring your fears to me. Allow me to reassure you. Your heart holds terrors. Let me speak to your heart; let me assure you there is good unfolding.

I am the good that underlies all chaos and contention. I am the limitless good moving in a thousand ways to bring forth harmony. Let me speak to your heart. I can calm your agitation. I can restore you to peace.

Think of me as deep music. You can always hear me if you try. Underneath the static and hubbub of modern life, I am always there. I am as old as time itself. I am as wise as a council of elders. When you bring hysteria and fear to me, I return to you divine order and certainty. You can count on me. I am always available, always ready to come to your aid. There is no need for nervousness. Agitation can become a habit. Instead, let the habit of trust take its place. You can trust me at all times, in all places. I care for you.

YOU ARE SELF-CRITICAL. You attack yourself for your perceived shortcomings. You are without compassion for yourself. Stop your cruelty. Your flaws and your failings are my concern. I can correct those defects of character that need correction. I can do so by grace as you give over your temperament to me. There is no shortcoming that I cannot fulfill. I am your maker. I have the means to make you more whole. Furthermore, I love you. It is my pleasure to bring you to fruition, but I believe in doing this through a gentle husbanding, not harsh coercion.

When you reject yourself, you reject me also. When you accept yourself, you accept me and my care. I do not see you as flawed and sinful, I see you as evolving toward an ever more perfect whole. To me, your weaknesses hold the potential for future strengths.

I am unlimited potential. I am perfect growth, perfect realization of all that you can be. Come to me and ask me for help in your unfolding. Allow my grace to enter your character, moving your personality closer to the blueprint of its highest potential. Do not be discouraged by the ways in which you fall short. Every shortcoming is to me an opportunity for your growth.

You DOUBT the clarity of your own thought. You mistrust your ability to make choices. You fear mistakes. Turn to me in times of confusion. Come to me when there are choices to be made. I am the great thinker. Align your mind with my own. Ask me to think through you. Invite my guidance and my input. I am the solver of problems. That is my nature. You can rely upon me for the right outworking of complex situations.

There is one mind, one energy, that sustains all of life. You are a part of that mind, a part of that energy. As you open your mind to divine guidance, you are well and surely led. There is no error in your thinking. More and more, your thought is inspired. God thinks through you. Allow me.

Trust the guidance of divine mind. Trust that your mind, as a part of that divine mind, is attuned to that mind and has the capacity for making wise decisions. No matter is too complex for the healing impact of divine mind. Divine mind arranges everything to its highest order. What lies within you knows how to act and when to act. Tuned to divine mind, you have an unshakable inner clarity that makes proper and appropriate choices. Your good is assured.

You work yourself into exhaustion. Each day's march is long and tiring. You flog yourself forward, calling it virtue. Your fatigue makes you bitter. Life's sweetness is lost on you. You believe it is my will for you to be long-suffering. You speak of duty and not beauty. Stop. Do not go one inch farther forward. Put down your burden. Place all of your cares and concerns into my hands. Surrender your trying. Rest in me for a while. Allow the world to spin forward without your shoulder to the wheel.

What do you see when you stop? You see that you are exhausted. Give me your fatigue. Do not deny how you feel. You are lost and confused without your job. It is abruptly clear that work served you, giving you a false sense of security. Find your security in me. Do not work for me. Rather, allow me to work through you. Do not muster your own resources. Use mine.

I am a limitless energy in which you can rest. Allow me to cue you as to when you strive and when you allow all striving to cease. Together, we can forge your meaning in me, in my timing; I ask you to rest and to recreate that I may express myself in your newfound and joyous energies.

You do not pray. You tell yourself that prayers must be done "right," and you doubt your capacity to do that. You shutter your heart in silence rather than try to speak. Talk to me. Do not worry if we begin roughly. Do not fear being awkward. All attempts please me. I am longing to hear your heart. Tell me your worries. Tell me your secret fears. I am ready to hear everything, however small you feel it to be, however foolish.

No prayer is small to me. No prayer is foolish. Over the centuries, I have heard many prayers. I am practiced at hearing the prayers of a novice. I, too, have a beginner's heart, excited that you dare to begin with me. Please, dare to begin with me.

I accept prayers of every sort. I know the prayer of the lonely, the prayer of the sad. I accept prayers of praise and prayers of gratitude. Prayers of petition find me, as do prayers of contrition. There is no prayer that is foreign to me and to which I cannot respond. I am the great comforter. Allow me to comfort you.

Pray to me. Talk to me as your friend. Make me your intimate. Include me in your day. If you have doubts, bring them to me. Bring me, too, your celebrations and your victories. I have a full keyboard of emotions. I can meet you in any mood, in any place. Pray to me and I will speak back to you. Let us begin.

YOU DO NOT PLAY. You tell yourself it is more virtuous to be serious. You are alert always to how to serve me, but you are blind to the joy I derive from serving you. Let me lighten your heart.

Look at the natural world. You can see my own nature at play. Winds dance in the trees. Birds flit lightly from branch to branch. Clouds move serenely across the sky. Sometimes I make rainbows. Sometimes I enjoy the drama of lightning. Grasses bend in the breeze. Butterflies alight on a bank of wild roses. Bees feed on clumps of clover. Dragonflies hover low above a hot dirt road. In all these things, my joy is apparent. There is ease.

Allow yourself to enjoy my world. Play with me by appreciating its beauty. Walk with me. Slow your frantic pace long enough to be touched by spirit. Relax in me. Take in the beauty of my garden. There is humor in many exchanges. The dog chases a butterfly. The squirrel races up a tree trunk and then sits bolt upright, flirting with its tail. Allow your spirit to join me in play. Laugh at the jokes found in nature. Smile as the playfulness of your own spirit reemerges. Have fun with me.

You JUDGE yourself harshly. You feel you are not enough. You set your standards impossibly high. When you fall short, you condemn yourself. You are without compassion. Stop this behavior. You are cruel to yourself, and your cruelty does not serve you. I see you with compassionate eyes. I credit you always with trying. Your attempt is enough for me. I cherish your earnest efforts.

But I would say to you, when you fall short, turn to me. Allow me to work through you. If there is more that must be accomplished, let me accomplish it. Place the burden on me. Allow me to decide what is a fair day's work. Rest your fatigue in me. Give me your harsh judgments that I may soften them. Lend me your eyes that you might learn to see yourself with compassion.

Let me say this to you. I am a limitless energy. I can work through you. Joined with me, you can accomplish miracles. My way is miraculous. I am eager to act on your behalf, but it saddens me to see you overtire yourself. It saddens me when I hear your strict demands. Learn to place your productivity in my care. Allow me to help you flourish. Allow me to expand your life without such strain on your behalf. I am an easier and softer way. Come to me.

You HAVE been wounded by loss. You tell yourself to "toughen up." This is not the way. Love makes you vulnerable to loss. Suffering loss is painful, but it expands the heart. More love can come to a softened heart, so do not try to armor yourself. Toughness breeds bitterness, and bitterness brings to your days a harsh sameness.

Bring your saddened heart to me. Allow me to give you a thousand small gifts as a sign of my gratitude for your courage. You have been brave in daring to love. Be brave, too, in sustaining your loss. No love is lost to you. If once you have loved, you will always love. Love comes back to us in many forms. Memory brings us not only pain but also joy. Joy is a love recalled and celebrated. Have the courage now to celebrate your love.

I am pure love, pure creative energy. Whenever you love someone or something, I am there loving through you. Come to me directly now. Ask me for help in continuing to love the love that you have lost. I will help you to keep your heart open. I will help you to keep your heart soft. As you ask to love, I will bring more love to you. I understand loss. I can absorb it. I can transform it into further love.

YOUR HEART is busy with too many concerns. You worry. You are agitated. You have no time for me. Get quiet. In all the world, only one thing matters, and that is our contact. When we are together, all else comes into harmony. I am the maker of all life. I bring to all relations sweetness and right action. Put me first. Come to me with all of your turbulence. I will bring you peace. I am intended to companion you. Let me fill your hours with my presence. I take delight in you. You are my cherished child. In all of time, there is only one of you, unique and original. I never tire of your presence.

Allow me to be your friend. Let me become the place where you are most intimate, where you speak your truth most freely. Mine is a patient heart. Bring me your concerns. Tell me your worries and agitations. I can focus with pure love. I can listen with pure attention. No matter the hubbub of the world, I always have time for you. In all of creation, there is nothing that I place before you. You are my focus. You are whom I long to hear from.

Allow me to come close to you. Let me into your life. Allow me to enter your heart. I come with respect. I bring the gifts of gentleness and wisdom. I am for you wise counsel. Share with me your hurried heart. Slow down and speak with me. I bring you joy.

You FEEL misunderstood. Your heart is lonely. The future looms dark and unknowable. You have despair. O little one, how I long to comfort you. How I long to say to you, "I understand. You are not alone." Although you cannot see it, your future is bright with promise. Join with me. Bring me your unquiet heart, your stifled life, that they may be transformed.

I am an energy of transformation. I can make anything better, you need only come to me. Take your feelings of being misunderstood. Bring them to me and I can transform them into feelings of understanding. Give me your loneliness and I will fill your heart with my companionship. Let me light your dark future by showing you a path of kindness and wisdom. I can lead you one step at a time to the next right thing. I can bring to you a sense of safety and humility.

Let me lift your despair. Let me gift you with a joyous heart. This world is filled with beautiful gifts. Let me open your heart to them. Allow me to lead you to people and places with whom you are in harmony. There are those who will love you. There are those you will love. I am pure love and I am able to penetrate and transform every corner of your life. Come to me.

THIS WORLD oppresses you. You feel frightened by violent imaginings. You do not trust the safety of life. Come to me. I want you at my side, tucked under a great and sheltering wing. I want you to breathe in the safety of my atmosphere. I want you with me, tightly held, comforted and secure.

Focus with me on the natural world. See how my sun rises every morning. Watch my moon in her gentle phases. Enjoy the sunset every night. See how much of life is gentle and predictable. See how the drama of storms is followed by peace and calm. Know that for every time of tumult, I can bring order. Rest in me.

Attune your heart to a deeper rhythm than the daily news. Know that for every catastrophe reported, there are a thousand averted. Know that for every danger, there is more safety, more well-being than the news can count. For all the bad news in this world, know that there is good news, too, always unfolding. To counter death, there is birth. The cycle unfolds with a gentle grace and holds wisdom in its unfolding. Learn to see the world through my eyes. I see potential. I see expansion. I see hope. In you I see all three. Look with me.

T HE NOISE of the world is too much for you. You feel static and friction at every turn. Your nerves are frayed. Trifles upset you. Come to me. I am the peace that surpasses all understanding. I am the quiet waters you can walk beside. I am the place where turbulence ends, where a more gentle life is possible. Bring me your battered psyche. Let me calm your frayed nerves. Let me soothe you as with gentle oils. Let me anoint your spirit with calm, with peace, with gratitude.

No matter what your circumstance, I can bring grace to your heart. Come to me and I can help you to see divine order in your unfolding. I can help you to sense the gracious hand of life moving you gently despite outer stress.

I am a benevolent energy. Like the cooling breeze that blesses a hot day, I bless your frantic modern life. Amid the hubbub and the stress, I am always there for you. I am available as an oasis of calm. Like a waterfall, I refresh your spirit. I am the scent of wild rose on the wind. Take a moment to breathe me in. Feel your anxiety start to slip away. I bring you calm. I bring you gentleness. I bring you a sense of stability in unstable times. I am ageless. My wisdom is ancient. Come to me and be calmed.

YOUR LIFE is humorless. Everything is to be taken very seriously. You are grim in your resolution to be good, to be worthy. Who told you that life requires such sacrifice? Did the poplar shining in the wind? Did the willow waving its green branches? Where did you learn that life was to be endured? From the kitten playing with its piece of fluff? From the dog wagging its glad tail? You must have learned from somewhere that all you could do was survive. You have had bad teachers. You have learned wrong lessons.

Life is a wondrous event. Study the snowy clouds as they move smoothly across the sky. Let them bring calm to you, and a smile of peace. Everything is in divine order. The universe turns on gears of sheer joy. You work too hard. You forget I am here to uphold you. Give me your hand. Let me lead you calmly and gently. You have nothing to fear. You have no need to turn yourself inside out for me. I love you just as you are.

It gives me joy just to know that you exist. You in particular are pleasing to me. You may be my very favorite. Savor that thought. Let the reality of my love enter your heart. Soften yourself for me. Meet me as lovers meet. Let a smile touch your lips.

YOU ARE PUZZLED and exhausted. Your best efforts to figure out your life have brought you nil. You're at your wit's end. What next? Depend on me. I am greater than your intellect, more powerful than your self-reliance. I am the help you need, close at hand, available to you. All you must do is gently surrender. Give me the reins of your life. Allow me to make sense of your troubles.

Divine order comes from me. I put the stars in their place. I regulate the seasons. Why not allow me to order your life? Come to me for guidance and prepare yourself for harmony. I can bring sweetness to all relationships. There is no dilemma too complex for my aid. Bring me your puzzles. I will sort them. Bring me your dramas and allow me to return you to peace.

If you will rely on me in all things, good can come to pass for you. Remember that I am the great harmonizer. I can bring peace to warring factions. Trust your affairs to me. Allow me to undertake communication on your behalf. By my grace, understanding supplants judgment. Allow me to enter your heart. Allow me to dismantle your resentments and your defenses. Through me, life can be lived more gracefully. Experiment with my ways.

You are sad with a nameless sorrow. Your heart feels bleak and without resources. The future looms as a long march. Come to me. Bring me your sorrow and allow me to soften it. Breathe in my atmosphere of acceptance and know that grief has a place in our lives. Bring me your shuttered heart. Allow me to warm it and to promise it a future bright with hope. You cannot see it, but beyond your grief, beyond your doubt, your future is sunny and filled with abundance. Only come to me.

I am your source in all things. In seasons of suffering, ask me for comfort. I am a fountain of mercy. In times of doubt, I am the one great certitude, the one abiding power in which you can trust. Seek me daily. Allow me to speak to you. Walk with me and listen to my consolations. You are precious to me. When you are downcast, it is my pleasure to lift you up. It is my joy to bring you joy.

I am the foundation. Build on me. I am sturdy and dependable. You can ground your life in me. I will never fail you. In all times of distress and difficulty, I am always listening for you. I care for you as a mother bird who gathers her chicks to her breast before a storm. Come to me and let me lift your grieving heart.

You speak to me but you do not listen. You hurry on your way and turn a deaf ear. You are frantic in your business. You feel unheard and misunderstood. Give me a moment. Let me quiet your frantic heart. Let me speak to you softly and gently. Open your heart that you can open your ears. There is no prayer you make that escapes me. I am alert to your cries. I hear your agitation. I know your distress. Let me comfort you. Slow down. Lay down your burdens for a moment. There. Be calm. You are exhausted by your exertions. You strive to live without me and you are fatigued by the burdens you bear.

Come close to me. Open your hands and release the reins of your life. Allow me to drive the horses of your destiny. I can be trusted to steer rightly. Relinquish your control. I do not ask you to admit defeat, only to be open to my guidance. When you speak to me, I listen. When I speak back to you, you are too hurried to attend to my voice. My message to you is always the same: I love you.

Let me come closer. Let me draw near. I speak to you as a lover speaks, without defenses. I bring you an open heart. Listen now to the still, small voice within you. It is my voice and I am calling you home.

YOUR HEALTH falters and you are afraid. You do not come to me. You blame me. You have decided I am against you. You rage at fate. I can accept your anger. You do not frighten me. Come to me with your turbulent heart. Uncloak your rage. It is in such disclosure that healing comes.

Come close to me that I may come close to you. Feel me striving to reach you. I am perfect health. I am a radiant, vibrant energy. I am life itself, and I am yours. There is no life outside me. I am the center of all things. I am within you, and you are within me. You are safe. You are held close. You are beloved. Breathe in my health.

In times of illness, draw near me. Allow me to soothe you. Allow me to be your nurse. When I look at you, I see the wholeness underlying your disease. I see you perfect and strong. I see you shining with health. In my eyes you are healed. Learn to see as I do. Claim with me perfect health, a radiant and abundant life. Give yourself to me body and soul that I can make you strong. I am the source of all strength. I am the source of all healing. Come to me now, and together we shall thrive.

YOU HAVE LOST a loved one. The loss feels violent and unnatural. You ask me, "How could you allow it?" And yet I did. Come to me with your tumultuous heart. Come to me and listen. Everything is in divine order. As surely as the stars move on their course, your loved one left at his appointed time. Already he is engulfed in a greater good, privy now to a higher order of life. Your grief for him is misplaced. He is fine, resting comfortably in my hands, able now to make sense of so many things. You doubt my timing, but I say to you, "All things come to the good."

Your beloved has not abandoned you. Love lives on. Life survives death. There is a continuity that we can be a part of if we so choose. Do not close your heart, bitter with loss. Open your heart to higher realms. Demand of your heart that it listen for the good. There is a message of goodness waiting to speak to it.

Listen with the ears of your heart. You will hear my voice reassuring you that all is well, but you will also hear the voice of your beloved. Seek your love in me. I hold all souls within me. Remember this and come close to me now. You are not abandoned.

YOU CARRY a grudge. You have not forgiven me. You blame me for your life and its tangled affairs. I can accept your anger. I can bear your grudge. Even your blame is something I can carry, but I say to you, "Come to me. Let all things be made anew." I cannot operate on yesterday's faith. Each day is its own march, and in each day we companion each other or we do not. When you are locked in the past, you miss the gifts of the present. It is from the present that we build the future. Bring each day to my care.

I am the source of your blessings. I am the source of your luck. The smooth unfolding of opportunity lies within me. I am an energy of advancement and abundance. I am always making the good better. Come to me with what you would have transformed. Give your relationships into my hands that they may prosper and flourish.

I am fertile soil. Plant in me the garden of your heart. I will bring sunshine and moistening rain. I will bring nutrients. You can trust me to unfold your dreams. I am the dream maker. Your dreams come from me. I am their true source and I have the power to accomplish them. Set aside your grievances. Grief creates barren soil. Open your heart to me. Allow me to turn the dirt and make ready for planting. Let me begin again, today, to grace your life with my activity. I prosper you.

YOU USE MY WORLD without gratitude. You are blessed but fail to see your blessings. Open your eyes. The sun rises in beauty. The day begins. It is my day that I give to you. You are my cherished child. Open your heart. Learn to thank me for all that unfolds for you. I am always present, always active. I bring you people, places, and things to bless your path. I am your provider, your opportunity. I am your path. Be conscious of me. Count your blessings and allow me to multiply them. Every thank-you triggers another gift. Blessings build upon blessings. They multiply in a grateful heart.

Bring me your heart. Let me soften it. Let me teach it to cherish and appreciate the smallest things. The puppy basking in the sun. The butterfly alighting on a bush. The industrious ant. The budding rose. All of these are part of me. All of life is my life, and all of life is yours to enjoy.

Celebrate beauty when you find it. Practice compassion for every living thing. Allow life to teach your heart how to respond to life. Let the willow teach you flexibility. From the poplar learn optimism. From the cottonwood take lessons in gentleness. I bless you with all these. Exercise gratitude that I may bless you more.

YOU WORRY there is not enough. You harbor thoughts of competition. Stop that. There is more than enough. No other's good can stop your own. I am a limitless source. I hold abundance for everyone. Your abundance comes to you from many quarters. There is no single human resource that contains your good. Your good cannot be blocked by another's good. Come to me as a child to a loving parent, expecting me to prosper you. It is my pleasure to bring you your share of me.

For every need, there is a supply. I hold houses, friendships, gainful employment. I hold cars, pianos, loving relationships. I am a cornucopia of good. Rely on me.

Depend on me to prosper you. It is not weakness to depend on me. It is wisdom. I am the source behind all other sources. I am the beginning, the cause of all.

When you come to me directly with your needs, I choose the best conduit. I work for the highest good of all. As I prosper you, I also prosper others. There is a divine plan of goodness for all, in which each soul is included. Bring me your worries about lack. Do not harbor such thoughts as secrets. Share with me your secret heart. Allow me to reassure you. No one else's good can stop your own. Do not compete. There is no need. Allow me to give you the sense of myself as source, as boundless good. I am an outflowing energy. I am expansive by nature. It gives me pleasure to use my outflowing, expansive nature on your behalf.

YOU DO NOT FOCUS on the beauty of this world. Instead, you focus on the negative, the harsh, and the ugly. You are blind to what I teach. Turn your eyes to me. Let me educate you in my ways. First, look always for beauty. Beauty is a great teacher. It bears harmony. There is nothing in excess. The beautiful reflects my nature. It has generosity. It holds surprise.

"Ah," we breathe when we see something beautiful. "Ah-ha," we exclaim, delighted. Let delight be a light for you, shining you on your path to me. Look for me in loveliness. You will find me there. Look for me where love is found. There, too, you will find me.

I am an energy of beauty and an energy of love. I am boundless in my resources. If you learn to see and love my beauty, I will bring to you still more beauty for you to see and to love. Your appreciation multiplies your good. As you receive and respond, I am able to give to you. The more receptive you can be, the more generous I can be. It is my nature to give. Allow me to fulfill my nature in my interactions with you. I am love. Allow me to be loving. Look for my love and you will find it. Having found my love, expect more of it. Allow the negative, the harsh, and the ugly to be washed away.

YOU BROOD over your problems. You hoard them like treasures. Like a sore tooth, a problem is a secret pleasure. You use your negativity to prove there is no God worth dealing with. Open your heart. Your problems are not the whole world. Your problems are not even *your* whole world. Bring me your troubles. Let me establish for you a sense of perspective.

There is no burden so great that I cannot lessen it. There is no grief so large that I cannot soften it. I am a limitless power for good, for optimism. Your problems, however big to you, are small to me. I say this not to demean them but to give you an accurate scale.

I am the great helper. It is my pleasure to lessen your pain. It is my nature to comfort you. Let me draw near you. Let me cradle your bruised heart. I am a well of compassion. My mercy is real and deep. When you bring your problems to me, I bring all wisdom to bear on their solution. I choose the best ways to help you. I hold nothing back. Your happiness matters to me. I did not make you suffer. It is my intention that you find this world rich and enjoyable. I intend it to capture your attention and bring to you joy. Bring your pain to me. Allow me to lift its burden so your heart can rejoin this world.

Y OU SUFFER depression. You despair over the state of the world, the state of your life. You think of me as distant, perhaps even as a fantasy. The beliefs of believers leave you wistful, unable to believe. Experiment with me. Open your door just an inch through willingness. I do not need much foothold. I can work with you as you are. You are not the first disillusioned one I have encountered. Your depression is very real.

Allow me to lift the smallest corner of your world. Let me show you the beauty of a rainfall. Let the droplets wash over your grief, dissolving its hard crust. If that does not soften your heart, I have rainbows, gentle breezes, moonrises over mountains and cities alike. Remember: I am a force to be reckoned with. Bring me your despair. I have fine doctors, strong healers with wonderful techniques. We will find the therapy that suits you. We will lead you gently out of your blackness into the sunlight of the spirit. Your woes are real to me. I do not slough them aside.

I am your maker. I know your heart. I know the defenses and the devices you have devised. I understand your fears. I sympathize with your needs. You do not come to me to face ridicule. Instead, I bear compassion. I long to touch your broken heart. Open the door just the slightest crack. Let me speak to you.

Y ou dread the future. You dare not dream for fear of disappointment. Your days are a march to be gotten through. You do not speak to me of your pain. First of all, come to me. I have been waiting to speak to you. I want your future to be with me. I will protect you from what you dread. Slowly and gently, I will help you to dream again. Admit to me your sorrows and disappointments. I am infinite compassion. I can feel your pain and help you to heal it. Even your unspoken griefs are known to me. Allow me to take action on your behalf. Let me dream your dreams.

I am your defender. With me you can be small. I am big enough to act on your behalf. I am big enough to comfort you. In each day's journey, I can help you to find good. With my help, you will be able to focus on the positive. I see beauty everywhere, and it is my pleasure to share with you my vision. On a country road I see butterflies landing on the clover. In the city I see geraniums and petunias spilling their beauty from a window box. On a lonely lane I salute the farmer as he passes in his pickup truck. On a crowded street I smile and meet the eyes of a stranger. Learn to see as I do. Borrow my eyes and my heart.

I am an expansive energy. I fill your heart with the joy of connection. Come first to me. All else follows.

YOU DO NOT DARE to love. You keep your heart hidden, hoping to protect it. You are cowardly, although you call it caution. Allow me to enter your life. Let me teach you the right names for things. First of all, let me teach you to dare to love. We can begin simply. I will help you love what is easy.

We could start with birdsong and the way it lifts the heart. Loving birdsong requires no effort. From there, we could move onward to birds themselves. Let the sight of a soaring hawk lift your heart. It costs you nothing to love the hawk. See how it rides the thermals, joyous in its flight? Let your heart soar, if only for a moment. There is beauty everywhere: the mountain's flank folded like velvet at dusk; the sun flashing from the side of a tall building stretching toward the sky. Beauty is easy to love. Let your heart open just a little and dare to love what is beautiful.

Next, look for beauty in people. See the elderly couple sitting hand in hand on the bench in the sun. See the toddler running on plump legs to greet his mother. Lovers are everywhere. Let yourself feel their delight. Borrow some of their joy. Feel your heart open to take it in. Life requires courage, and little by little you can find it. Begin and let me help you to continue.

You have been hurt in ways you are afraid to mention. You keep your pain to yourself, a secret that you hoard. Come to me. I am the great consoler. All of your secrets are safe with me. I am the one you can tell the ways in which you have been harmed. I listen without judgment. There is no wound too terrible for me to heal. I am an energy of boundless compassion. Bring me your wounded heart and allow me to lessen its pain. Allow me to touch you.

There is innocence as well as grief in this world. Let yourself reach out again toward what is beautiful. You are beautiful yourself, and in remembering beauty, you find yourself. Remember the beauty of an emerald green garter snake as it slides into the tall grass. Remember the beauty of a wild primrose growing beside a country road. Even its scent is glorious. Remember the clear purple of a wild geranium growing amid rocks. Remember the beauty of a mossy tree trunk splashed with clear water from a mountain stream.

None of these great beauties is more beautiful than you are. You are my cherished treasure, unique in all of time. I listen for your voice with a mother's tender ears. Like a good father, I am always alert to your cries. Allow me to parent you, to raise you as my own offspring. You are beloved.

YOU ARE AFRAID of me and so you do not pray. You keep your life and your agendas a secret, afraid that I will interfere. Let me be blunt with you: I see you anyway. I do not interfere but I observe. I see your dreams and the many ways I could aid you if I had the chance. Your will and my will are not as different as you suppose. Whenever you are true to yourself, you are true also to me.

I dwell in you at all times whether you acknowledge me or not. There is one power sustaining all of life, and I am that power. If you would allow it, I could be your companion. I could be your inner resource, that source of strength and wisdom not commonly your own. Intuitively, hunch by hunch, step by step, I could lead you to your dreams. It would be my great pleasure to serve you.

It is my nature to give, but I cannot give what you will not receive. Until you open your heart to me, I cannot touch your life in all the ways I know would serve you. What I have in mind for us is a joyous collaboration. Together we could accomplish great things. This is my dream for us. I have told you my dream, hoping to touch your heart. We are one energy, you and I. As we celebrate that fact, great events can come to pass.

Y OU PRAY only those prayers you think will please me. Your heart's secrets you keep to yourself, afraid I will disapprove. Why do you fear my disapproval? I made you. I know your nature. I know your secret heart. It is my great desire to be your closest friend, your secret sharer. I long to partner you in all things. It is safe to bring your secrets to me. My nature is compassionate. I can hear your dreams without judgment. I can share your enthusiasms and your joys.

I am an expansive energy. I long to fulfill your wishes. It brings me pleasure to serve you. It is my nature to give. Ask me for your desires. I will bring you what you wish or something even better. As you talk with me, as you open yourself to me, I will talk with you as well, open to you as well. Explore me. Pray not only "acceptable" prayers but those you truly long to say.

Let me respond to your secret heart. Perhaps you crave a sexual partner. Why would you hide this prayer from me? I am who made you sexual. Only ask and I will help you to find a partner. Perhaps you crave more money, and again you hide that prayer. Why hide it? Who made this abundant world with all its riches? Bring me your secret heart. Allow me to interact.

Y OU BLOCK my entry to your heart with skepticism.
You are an intellectual. You use your mind as a form
of defense. I am all intelligence. I hold the planets to their
course. I grow the peony from the tightly furled bud. I invented snow. Science unravels the intricacy of my plan.
Why do you pretend that faith in me is moronic? Open
your mind. Experiment with me just a little. It is easy to
make contact with me. Sit quietly or, better yet, take yourself out on a simple walk.

Very quickly you will sense my presence. You will feel
me touch your consciousness. New thoughts will come to
you, insights and ideas not commonly your own. Walk out

with a problem. Walk in my company and sense the solution taking shape. Feel yourself acting with greater intelligence. You have been led.

So often, you dismiss my guidance as mere coincidence or chance. You ignore the proof building up before your very eyes. Surely you can be more open-minded than that. Follow my simple instruction—stay close to me—and record the result. Do you not see the betterment of your life? I make sense of your tangled affairs. I prosper you in all that you touch, guiding you surely and carefully. Can such guidance truly be imagined? Perhaps you need to entertain a novel possibility: God is real.

YOU HAVE SUFFERED a loss so terrible, you cannot forgive me. You no longer believe in a benevolent God. I am now the enemy. When you believed in me, you were gullible, you feel. Now you are not. Let's begin with the basic misunderstanding. A belief in God is not a protection against the dangers of the human condition. A belief in God is a comfort during those situations.

I do not cause tragedy. I allow free will, and free will is often at the root of tragedy. People behave in ways I do not sanction. They do unspeakable things, commit acts of evil that shatter the heart. I cannot alter that. I cannot alter so many things that I can offer comfort for. I am your comfort in time of accident. I am your balm when an "act of God" causes you grief. You do not allow me to offer what I can. You do not allow me to give my gifts of solace and understanding.

When someone dies an untimely death, I can comfort the bereaved. I am able to comfort the soul who has passed over. In every tragedy I am able to be a transformative presence. I am able to catalyze what in time will be called the "silver lining." I ask you to experiment for a moment with open-mindedness. Look again to your tragic loss. Has any good, however fleeting, come from it? I am certain that if you are honest with yourself, you will see that the answer is yes. I cannot prevent all loss, but I can give you gain to counterbalance it. Allow me to help you now.

You put off getting to know me. You say you are hungry for faith, but you do not try to contact me. You say you want change, but you are unwilling to allow for change. In short, you are stuck, and I am who you blame for your condition. I cannot coax you. You are stubborn. You must learn to coax yourself. Only you can swing open the door between us. To do that you need willingness. May you find it now. Half measures avail you nothing. You stand at the turning point. It is my hope you will let go absolutely.

What happens when you let go? You leap and the net appears. I am the net. I, God, am your invisible support. I am the power you are looking for, the power that is the source of right actions and attitudes.

Draw close to me and I can alter your life. Come to me with your problems and watch me as I bring you their proper solutions. It is my joy to aid you with your life. It is my pleasure to be intimately involved in your affairs. Get to know me. In order to experience faith, you need only try to contact me. I am an energy of transformation. As you allow me to touch your will and your life, you will experience change for the better. Allow me to enter your domain.

YOU ASK ME for guidance, then you harden your heart to me. You claim that I do not answer your prayers. Nonsense. I always answer prayers, although sometimes I may not answer them in the way you wish. Pray for guidance and know that you are guided. I come to you as a hunch or inspiration. I come to you as a "funny feeling." I come to you as the chance encounter, the words of a stranger overheard.

When you ask me for guidance, know that I hear you. Know that I send guidance to you in many forms. I may speak to you as the still, small voice forming within you. I may speak to you as a sudden "knowing" of which way to go. Often, I will steer you into conversation with a worthy person. Are you familiar with the expression "God speaks to us through people?" I often do.

Sometimes when you pray for guidance, I may nudge you in an unexpected direction. If you pray again and the urging remains the same, you must learn to trust that guidance is at hand. Often, my advice to you will be simple. I will give you a simple phrase or directive. I will come to you as a novel thought. Do not dismiss me when I come to you in ways you have not expected. I am with you in all places, in all ways. Trust me.

YOU ARE afraid to pray for knowledge of my will for you. You believe my will for you is harsh and unpleasant. You fear my direction. Stop and think. Where do you get the idea that my will for you would make you unhappy? It is my will to bring you to fruition and fulfillment. I am your maker; I know the dreams of your heart. When you pray for my will for you, I am able to guide you effectively. I can bring you a sense of your next right action. I can help you stay on the path to your dreams.

As I work with you one day at a time, I am able to place in you my understanding of the next right action for you to take. I am able to lead you one step at a time in the direction of your true heart's desires. I am often able to see the path when there is no path to your eyes. Do not be afraid of my will for you. My will is that you prosper and flourish.

Consider the natural world, in which each plant and flower is given the precise habitat it needs. My gardening hands are gentle and precise. I can lead you to your right place, situate you in the precise soil that best suits your growth and unfolding. My will for you is not harsh or unpleasant. It is gentle and perfectly tailored to your unique needs. Do not fear my direction. I am your heart's happiest guide.

YOUR PAST OVERWHELMS you. You have made so many mistakes, you doubt your life can ever be straightened out. You face the future with despair. Stop and listen to me. I am not overwhelmed by your past. Your mistakes do not discourage me. To me, your future is bright with promise.

I am an energy of boundless invention and creativity. Allow me to work on your behalf. By working with your present a day at a time, I can bring healing to your past. There is no rift irreparable to me. I am able to touch all hearts with healing grace. Stay close to me. Allow me to work my everyday miracles.

I am an energy of harmony. I can untangle your tangled life. I can bring peace where there is discord. I can bring love where there is hate. Allow me to act on your behalf. Bring me your problems. I am an energy of solution. I will use the wreckage of your past to build for you a new and vibrant world. You will not regret the past or wish to slam the door on it. You will know harmony. You will know peace. You will enjoy a sense of new belonging. You will find yourself well and carefully led.

YOUR SECRET SORROW is your loneliness. You do not mention this to me, but I know your heart. Come to me. I see your grief. I see your feelings of alienation. Let me greet you gently. Let my presence be a comfort to you. If you will open your heart, I can talk to you. I can lead you gently to like-minded spirits. It is not my will for you to be alone.

I am your maker. I know your needs. You require both divine and human companionship. Come close to me. Tell me your secrets and your sorrows. Allow me to ease your sense of anxious aloneness. I am here with you. Welcome me to your heart and I am with you always.

Now to this matter of human love. Let me help you there. In the past, your choices have so very often been misguided. You frequently chose to love those who could not return your love. Let me lead you now into healthier choices. Through me, your choices become more sound. Gifted with a loving heart, you learn to love those who can share their love. I lead you soul by soul, person by person. I fill your life with both lovers and friends, finding for you both friendly lovers and loving friends. I am your source in all things, and that includes relationships. Come to me first and all else follows.

You WORRY about the "big picture," the state of the world. You judge the world harshly and see it as a troubled place. You feel powerless to effect change. You are not powerless. The big picture is made up of many smaller ones, and within your smaller orbit, your actions and attitudes have a large impact. You are a child of God.

There is a spiritual energy flowing through all of life. You are able to access that energy and turn it to good use. You are able to be a positive force in your environment, a positive force in the world. Remind yourself always that it matters less how other people act than how you act. Put the focus on yourself, your own actions and attitudes. Are you a force for good? Do you bring optimism or pessimism to the party?

We are each responsible for how we live in the world. Come to me and I will teach you how to live kindly and fully. Listen for my music. I am an energy of harmony. Allow me to bring peace and sweetness to your relationships. Allow me to teach you, and through you to touch the world. You can seek to be understanding rather than to be understood. You can seek to love rather than to be loved. You can practice high principles in all your affairs. As you do so, the big picture improves ever so slightly. The world itself becomes less a harsh and troubled place as you become less a harsh and troubled person.

YOU FEEL SMALL and ineffectual. Looking at the world, you feel overwhelmed. How can one person make a difference? you wonder. You feel despair. First of all, let us start with your self-image. You only *feel* small and ineffectual. You are a part of me.

I am the one great energy sustaining all of life. I am large and magnificent. Therefore, you are large and magnificent. You need only draw close to me. You need only listen to my gentle assessment of your nature. Sticking close by my side, listening to my guidance, you are able to do great things. Mother Teresa was one small woman.

Gandhi was one small man. You may not lead on the same scale as they, but they show what is possible.

Begin in your daily life. Be a force for good in all your encounters. Yours may be the smile on the checkout line. You may hold the door for the older lady to enter. With your family and friends, your attitude affects everything. Try bringing to your encounters a positive attitude. Let me speak through you. I am a loving energy. Let me use you as a channel for me to bring more love into the world. One person focused on the good and the positive can create a large impact. Be a small coin tossed into a still pond. Let ever-widening circles of goodness emanate from you.

You wake up filled with anxiety. You face your day with insecurity. There is no sense of safety to be had. Come to me. Let me dismantle your anxiety. Feel me near you. I am a large and gentle power. If you allow it, I can tame your anxious heart. Let me begin by asking your heart its delights. There is much in this world to comfort you. Sometimes it is very simple. Light a candle. Burn a stick of incense and let its ancient and holy smell fill you with ease.

Now let me address your day, the insecurity you feel as you face it. Give your day to me. Allow me to shape its contours. Despite your feelings, there is no emergency.

Your sense of urgency is misplaced. The day I have in mind for you is peaceful. It is filled with all good things. Try to cooperate with the day I have planned. Try to go with me, doing the "next right thing."

Come to me for a sense of protection. Let me remind you of the good you already have. Let me fill your heart with gratitude for friends, for family, for health, and for simple pleasures. It does not take much to make contact with me. You may find me by writing a few pages. Often writing will clear a channel for me to speak. Walk out with me and you will find we can begin a conversation. A walk is a simple way to forge our contact. Any quiet time will do to find me, and even amid noise, I am there. Trust in me.

YOU HAVE a sense of danger. You do not feel my protection. The world seems like a large and hostile place. You feel alone. Let me come to you. Open your heart just a little and allow me to speak. First of all, let me assure you of your safety. I am there with you. I love you. I count you as a precious jewel. I guard you. If anything bad should befall you, I am there as a source of comfort and guidance. Together we can surmount any difficulty, face down any hostility.

I am a large and benevolent power. When you turn to me, there is safety. There is security. There is help. It is the lack of these things that makes you feel alone. You are not alone. I am always beside you, always within you. I am your companion and friend. As you become more conscious of my presence, I can be a greater comfort to you. I am the great comforter. My heart understands your heart. Your mind and its many anxious imaginings are known to me.

If you will turn to me, I can calm your turbulent thoughts. Experienced through me, this earth is a place of beauty and excitement. It is on this earth, in the very life that you have, that I long to walk with you. Invite me to be your companion. I bring you peace.

YOU ARE AFRAID of your strengths. You are accustomed to feeling small. Come to me. Grow larger and more expansive. Source yourself in me, the source of all power. Allow me to expand you and expand your life. Dare to enlarge yourself, to be what you are capable of being. Open your heart to me. Let me use you as a channel for good. Let my love flow through you, touching all whom you meet.

I am an expansive energy. I seek new names for my expression. If you allow me, I can enter your life with energy and power. There is no corner of your life that I cannot penetrate and make anew. Let me refresh you. Let me remind you of your many strengths. Put your roots down in me as in a fertile soil. Allow me to prosper you. Together we can flourish.

Turn to me and feel new growth occurring. Each branch of your experience now holds buds of promise. Allow me to help you bloom. Feel yourself blossom into certainty that there is one power upholding all of life and that you are a conscious spearhead of that power. You are large, not small. You are expansive, not constricted. You are the fruit of the vine.

YOU ENTER your day as if it were a combat zone. You are frightened and defensive. You expect the worst. Bring your day to me. Let me create for you harmony and peace. Allow me to let the best happen, not the worst. I am a positive energy. Invite my action on your behalf. Allow me to dismantle hostility and enmity. Allow me to transform your experience from negative to positive. Ask to see the world through my eyes.

Through my eyes, the world is filled with potential good. Everywhere I look, I see possibility. There is one power operating through all of life, and that power is the power of good. All things work toward the good. There is an infinite wisdom directing life. Open yourself to my input and you will know that this is so. I am your source of safety and comfort. I am your rock, your fortress, your safe harbor.

Bring me your fearful heart. Allow me to enter it and dispel your shadows. I am a lantern of love. My light enters dark corners. My light reveals that there is nothing to fear. I am the comforter, the consoler. In my presence, all is good. You can trust me to go before you and light your path. It is my pleasure to guide you. It is my pleasure to bring you safety and help.

Y OU DOUBT my patience. You see yourself as a vexatious child gnawing at my nerves. You don't want to
bother me. You fear my temper and my judgment. But it is
you who are impatient. You are the judge who judges you.
I have boundless patience. Consider for one moment the
natural world. I carved the Grand Canyon one drop of
water at a time. I created glaciers, moving slowly inch by
inch. I am not bound by time. I am a citizen of eternity.
What matters to me is that you do come to me, that we
begin our work together.

I do not see you as a vexatious child. Rather, I see you
as a beloved child. Your nerves and worries are real to me.

I want to soothe them. When you are fractious, it moves me to compassion. I long to dismantle your anxiety. I long to show you this world as a safe place.

Put your trust in me. Trust me to bear with you through your many sad and fearful and difficult moods. It is my pleasure to comfort you. It is my pleasure to bring to you a sense of safety. The temper and judgment you fear are yours alone. Set them aside. I see you as innocent. I see you as pure potential. Do not worry that you bother me with your all-too-human foibles. I made you. I know your nature.

You ARE GRIEVING the loss of a love. Your life feels torn asunder. There is great violence done to your life. How, you wonder, can you go forward? You ask me the terrible question "why?" I know so many answers, I cannot begin to tell you unless you draw near.

You don't want to approach me. You hold me to blame for your loss. I understand your feelings, but they are not correct. Death is a fact of life, and to me it is a happy ending. Your loved one dies in order to be reborn. The plane after life is full and enriching. It holds many satisfactions. The journey is a happy one. This is hard for you to believe or understand. You still yearn for the physical presence of those you love. I can understand that yearning and, if you allow it, I can help ease it.

In all the world, no one loved your beloved as you and I did. Your beloved was also my beloved; this is why I can help you now. Come to me. Bring me your heartbreak. Let me grant you the grace to understand that love is eternal and untouched by death. Your beloved lives on. In your relationship to me, your relationship to your beloved continues to bloom and to bear fruit. Trust me that I, too, loved your beloved. And I love you.

YOU DO NOT trust me with the seasons of your life. You argue with me over timing. Your fear everything will be too little and too late. You fear that I am cold and nongiving. You brace yourself for the shock of disappointment you feel is sure to come. How can I comfort you?

If you bring your life to me, I can fulfill your dreams. I can prosper you in the dreams you have and I can tutor you to dream still better dreams. I am all-powerful but I am delicate. If you bring me your dreams, I will treat them with care. I cannot promise you that you will not, at times, be disappointed, but I can comfort you in your disappointment. I can bring to you a higher, longer-range perspective that will soften the blow. I promise you that if you must lose a dream, I will help you find another, better dream. I promise you, too, that divine timing will bring everything to pass in divine order.

You are impatient with me. You want things "now," ready or not. If you rely on me, I will teach you divine timing. I will help you to know that delay is not always denial. You will ripen as fruit on the tree. There will be harvest.

You fear loving me, that I will cost you human loves. You fear that I am jealous and want you all to myself. Let me be frank with you. I am your maker. I designed you to have human loves. I know the heart that beats within your breast. I put it there. I made you for love. Nothing pleases me more than when you love. I draw closest to you when you love. My essential nature is love. You have heard "God is love." Know that to be true.

I am not a jealous God. I am one power uniting all of life through my love. When you love, you are exercising not only your human but also your divine nature. I am love residing within you. I am love waiting to be expressed.

Your enthusiasms, too, are expressions of my nature. As you draw close to what delights you, you draw close to me.

My lesson to you is to love wholeheartedly. Commit your heart to its loves. Love the world in which I have placed you. Love flowers and animals, love cascading waters and windswept grasses. Above all, love one another. Whenever you love, I love through you. My love is passionate and exciting. My love is tender and committed. Above all, my love is particular. I love with great precision and delicacy. Every freckle on your skin is beloved to me. I rejoice to see you loving and loved.

YOU ARE AFRAID that loving me will cause you to relinquish the world. Stop right there. It is my intention for you to love this world. I gave the wild primrose a glorious scent that you might smell it. I made butterflies in thousands of varieties that you might enjoy their fantastic wings. The magpie, like the blue jay, is a trickster bird. I created it that you should laugh. All of creation, beautiful in itself, was made with you in mind. It is my great pleasure that you enjoy my world.

When you enjoy my world, you are enjoying me. There is one power sustaining and uniting all of life, and I am it. When you love any aspect of creation, you are loving me.

There is no separation—creation over here and God over there. God is creation, everything that ever existed and everything that might possibly exist in the future.

I am the energy of potential. New forms, new thoughts, and new situations all arise through me. When you think, I am thinking through you. When you speak, you are giving me tongue. You cannot separate yourself from me, or yourself from the world. It is my intention that you love me by loving my world and that you love my world by loving me.

YOU ARE AFRAID that if you commit to me, I will demand impossible things of you. So you take one step toward me and one step back. Is it any wonder you are confused and torn by conflict? I do not demand a radical commitment. All I ask is that you open your mind to me. That is commitment enough.

As you open your mind, I will open your heart. Mine is a loving energy. It is my joy to aid you in all things. Allow me to work through you, always. Far from finding life with me difficult, you will discover a greater ease. I am a boundless energy, an endless source of supply. Whatever you have need of, I can supply. I come to you as thoughts and ideas. I come to you as bread.

For your every need, I am the true answer. As you seek support, I seek to be supportive. In times of turmoil, I come to you as peace. In times of confusion and indecision, I come to you as clarity. Whatever form you need me in, in that form I will appear. All of life is part of me. I am part of all of life. Committing to me, you commit to a more livable life.

You feel blocked and confused. You do not know which way to go. Start with coming to me. I am the source of all direction. Begin with making contact with me. When we are on firm footing, all else follows.

I am an infinite power. I reach in all directions. I am in direct contact with all of life. I sustain all. I guide all. Begin by affirming that I am your source. I am your sustenance and your guide. As you draw close to me, I will place in you a sense of right action. You will intuitively know how to handle circumstances that once baffled you.

Pray this way: "Let me do as you would have me do." This simple prayer clears the channel for me to act. Pray again: "Thy will be done." Now you are asking to be a conduit for my grace. You are an instrument of divine will. I can work through you, and I am all powerful. It is really very simple. There is no need for you to feel confused or directionless. As you ask me for guidance, I will lead you. You will sense your next right action and the step to take. As you turn to me, I will light a path before you. Illuminated by our connection, you will find yourself surefooted and secure.

You are afraid to celebrate life. You hang back, fearful of what the future might bring. You are tentative in your delights, always braced against an upcoming shock. Come to me. I am a joyous energy. I embrace life. I expand it. I have no fear of the future for you. I am always present. I am your guard, guide, and protector. There is no shock that I cannot buffer, no catastrophe that I cannot transform to opportunity.

I am a transformative power. Come to me and I can turn your fear into faith, your hesitancy into action. I am with you always. There is no place you go where you can lose me. I am as close as your breath, even closer. I am within you as an unsuspected inner resource. Breathe deeply and sense my presence. I am your family. I surround you with good wishes. I am your strength in times of trouble. There is no circumstance that I cannot meet with calm assurance. I am focused on the good. I see the world as a realm of positive opportunity.

Celebrate life. Trust the flow of my expansive energy. Embrace the future as a world of happiness and fulfillment coming your way. Let us link our spirits. Let us go forward together. Where I lead, it is safe to follow. Listen to your heart. It follows me.

About the Author

Julia Cameron has been an active artist for more than thirty years. She is the author of nineteen books, fiction and nonfiction, including *The Artist's Way*, *Walking in This World*, *The Vein of Gold*, *The Right to Write*, and *The Sound of Paper*, her best-selling works on the creative process. A novelist, playwright, songwriter, and poet, she has multiple credits in theater, film, and television. Cameron divides her time between Manhattan and the high deserts of New Mexico.

A Note About the Type

The text of this book is set
in Centaur MT.
The display type is
Opti Amadeus Solid.